Contents

Any words appearing in the text in bold, **like this**, are explained in the Glossary.

The many mysteries of space

Did you know that astronomers can see stars as they were 13 billion years ago? Or that some galaxies are racing away from us almost as fast as light? Or that the Universe began with a rumbling hum? These are just some of the amazing things that astronomers have discovered about the Universe.

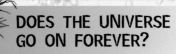

DOES THE UNIVERSE GO ON FOREVER?

People have been asking this question for thousands of years but still nobody knows. A Universe that stretches out forever is said to be infinite. Most scientists think our Universe is infinite. A Universe that has a limit is said to be finite. Some current research suggests that it might be finite after all – very, very big but finite.

Long ago, our ancestors looked up at the night sky. All they could see was twinkling stars. They saw some patterns in the stars, called constellations, and wove many wonderful stories around them. We still see the same stars shining above us if we look up at the sky now. But our understanding of the night sky has changed far beyond anything our ancestors could ever have imagined.

When we look up at the night sky we are gazing into space, and space contains unimaginably more than we can see with our eyes alone. Over the centuries, astronomers have probed further and further into space, using ever more powerful telescopes. They have also worked out theories that have helped them piece what they can see into a picture of the entire Universe.

The Universe is the whole of space and everything in it. The Universe contains over 100 billion galaxies (vast groups of stars), each containing as many as 100 billion stars like the Sun. Many of these stars have planets circling them, just as Earth circles the Sun.

From Ptolemy's Spheres to Dark Energy

www.heinemann.co.uk/library

Visit our website to find out more information about Heinemann Library books.

To order:

☎ Phone 44 (0) 1865 888066

🖹 Send a fax to 44 (0) 1865 314091

💻 Visit the Heinemann Bookshop at www.heinemann.co.uk/library to browse our catalogue and order online.

Produced for Heinemann Library by
White-Thomson Publishing Ltd,
Bridgewater Business Centre,
210 High Street,
Lewes, East Sussex BN7 2NH

First published in Great Britain by Heinemann Library,
Jordan Hill, Oxford OX2 8EJ, part of Harcourt Education.

Heinemann Library is a registered trademark of Harcourt
Education Ltd.

Consultant: Mike Goldsmith
Commissioning editors: Andrew Farrow and
    Steve White-Thomson
Editors: Kelly Davis and Richard Woodham
Proofreader: Catherine Clarke
Design: Tim Mayer
Picture research: Amy Sparks

Originated by RMW
Printed and bound in China by Leo Paper Group Ltd

ISBN 978-0-431-18661-0 (hardback)
11 10 09 08 07
10 9 8 7 6 5 4 3 2 1

ISBN 978-0-431-18668-9 (paperback)
12 11 10 09 08
10 9 8 7 6 5 4 3 2 1

British Library Cataloguing in Publication Data
Farndon, John
From Ptolemy's Spheres to Dark Energy: Discovering
the Universe
520.9

A full catalogue record for this book is available from the
British Library.

Acknowledgements
The author and publisher would like to thank the follow-
ing for allowing their pictures to be reproduced
in this publication: akg-images pp. 9, 11 (Erich Lessing),
12, 14 (Erich Lessing); Corbis pp. 8 (Dietrich Rose/zefa),
16 (Bettmann), 21 (Bettmann), 29 (Bettmann), 38
(Bettmann), 55 (Roger Ressmeyer); International
Space Station Imagery p. 25; NASA Center pp. 35;
Science Photo Library pp. 1(NOAO/AURA/NSF), 5
(Detlev van Ravenswaay), 7, 13 (NASA), 15 (David
Parker), 17 (Eckhard Slawik), 19 (David A. Hardy),
23 (Tony and Daphne Hallas), 26 (Volker Steger), 27
(Julian Baum), 28 (Roger Harris), 30 (David Parker), 32
(NOAO/AURA/NSF), 34 (Seymour), 37, 39 (Physics Today
Collection/American Institute of Physics), 41 (NASA), 43
(European Space Agency), 44 (Joe Tucciarone), 46
(Physics Today/American Institute of Physics), 47
(Yannick Mellier/IAP), 48 (Russell Kightley), 49 (Mark
Garlick), 50 (Philippe Plailly), 52 (NASA), 53 (NASA);
Topfoto.co.uk pp. 6 (Musée du Louvre, Paris/Pedro
Berruguete), 22, 24, 36.

Cover design by Tim Mayer.

Scientists have gradually gained a detailed understanding of the way the Universe is today. They have also traced its history back to the first fraction of a second after it came into being, in what is called the **Big Bang**.

Our knowledge of the Universe is increasing by the day. Yet the more we learn, the more mysterious we find it. Each time scientists think they have discovered most things, they find they have barely begun.

Scientists now think the Universe began from virtually nothing about 13.7 billion years ago, and has been swelling out at a fantastic rate ever since. This is called the Big Bang theory, and this picture is how an artist imagines the Big Bang.

THAT'S AMAZING!

We can see 5,000–10,000 stars without a telescope, but there are trillions more in space. There are also a number of planets, such as Earth, that circle the Sun. Five of these planets – Mercury, Venus, Mars, Jupiter, and Saturn – are easy to see without a telescope. These planets have no light of their own, but are so close that they reflect sunlight more brightly than all but the brightest stars shine. The brightest object of all is also the nearest to Earth – the Moon.

How the heavens move

Astronomy is a very ancient art. Both the Babylonians and ancient Egyptians made precise observations of the stars. Yet the earliest ideas about the Universe were myths. It was the Greeks and Romans who first studied the Universe scientifically.

The Greeks knew a surprising amount about the Universe. They worked out that Earth is round, from clues such as the way ships dip below the horizon. They also came up with the idea that the Sun and Moon are giant balls circling Earth far away. Using geometry, Greek thinkers even calculated roughly how far away and roughly how big the Sun and Moon are.

Based on all these ideas, two brilliant astronomers, the Greek Hipparchus (c.200–126 BC) and the Roman Ptolemy (c.AD 90–151), built up a remarkable model of how the Universe works. Their ideas, known as the **Ptolemaic system**, are contained in Ptolemy's book *Almagest*.

This is a 15th-century portrait of Ptolemy. After the Roman Empire collapsed, Ptolemy's ideas survived only in the Middle East. His ideas were finally brought back to Europe during the Middle Ages.

The Ptolemaic system

In the Ptolemaic system, Earth is the fixed centre of the Universe. Around Earth rotate vast transparent or "crystal" spheres. The crystal spheres carry the heavenly bodies with them. There is one sphere for the Sun, one for the Moon, one for the stars, and one for each planet.

The Ptolemaic system was not just a picture of the Universe. It was a mathematical machine for predicting the exact movements of the Sun, the Moon, the planets, and stars. Although it turned out to be wrong, it provided a good basis for astronomical calculations for more than 1,500 years.

The wanderers

The planets were a problem for Ptolemy because they do not simply move in a smooth curve through the sky. The Greeks called them planets, which is Greek for "wanderers". This is because they appear to loop backwards every now and then. This movement, now known as **retrograde motion**, is simply because of the way Earth moves past the planets. Yet, in the Ptolemaic system, Earth was fixed. To account for this seemingly strange, backward motion, Ptolemy had to invent an elaborate system of circles within circles called **epicycles**.

This is a rather fanciful 19th-century illustration of Ptolemy's crystal spheres. Yet Ptolemy's system allowed astronomers to predict the movements of the stars and the planets very precisely.

THAT'S AMAZING!

It was not until the 17th century that most scientists realized that Earth is not fixed, but circles around the Sun. However, the Greek thinker Aristarchus worked this out 2,000 years earlier. He suggested, correctly, that Earth circles the Sun, along with the planets, while the stars are far away. He even realized that we get night and day because Earth spins on its axis to face the Sun every 24 hours.

Moving Earth

Ptolemy's system seemed to work so well that for 1,400 years no one questioned whether it was right. For the powerful Roman Catholic Church, it seemed exactly as it should be that Earth was the centre of the Universe. Then, around 1500, a Polish priest, Nicolaus Copernicus (1473–1543), proposed some other ideas.

The German astronomer Regiomontanus (1436–1476) wrote a summary of Ptolemy's system. He added a pamphlet called *Epitome* in 1462, in which he pointed out a few problems. For instance, to him, the way Ptolemy explained how the Moon moved did not seem to work.

For much of his life, Copernicus was a priest at the cathedral of Frombork in Poland. He often climbed the cathedral tower to study the night sky – and these night climbs may have inspired his ideas about the Universe.

Copernicus read *Epitome* and it set him thinking. Ptolemy's system seemed too elaborate. Surely, Copernicus felt, God would have created something simpler? Yet it was only because Earth was fixed at the centre that Ptolemy needed such a complicated system to account for the movement of the planets. Copernicus saw that if the Sun is at the centre, and Earth revolves around it along with all the planets, most of the complications vanish.

In 1514, Copernicus wrote a little book called *Commentariolus*. In this book, he laid out his ideas about a Sun-centred Universe. He showed how this explained the planets' **retrograde motion**. He also argued that the stars are very far away, and they only appear to move because Earth is turning.

This illustration shows Copernicus' theory, which put the Sun at the centre of the Universe. You can see the Moon orbiting Earth at the top, in the centre.

Copernicus put his theories in a great book, called *De revolutionibus orbium coelestium* ("On the revolutions of the heavenly spheres"), published around the time of his death in 1543. Yet it was more than a century before his ideas were widely accepted. Europe was going through religious turmoil at the time, with Protestants breaking away from the Catholics. The last thing the Catholic Church wanted was a challenge to their most basic ideas.

The Solar System

Copernicus was groping his way towards what we now know to be true. Earth is part of the **Solar System**. The Solar System is made up of the Sun, along with the planets and various smaller objects, such as **asteroids**, that continually orbit (circle) it. Our Solar System is one of countless similar systems in the Universe.

WHO WAS THE FIRST PERSON TO USE A TELESCOPE FOR ASTRONOMY?

An English gentleman called Thomas Digges (1546–1595) was probably the first person to use a very crude version of a telescope for astronomy. Digges was an early champion of Copernicus' Sun-centred view of the Universe. In fact, he went even further than Copernicus. He argued that the Universe around the Solar System is infinite, with a multitude of stars in all directions.

Kepler's ovals

The famous Danish astronomer Tycho Brahe (1546–1601) was well aware of Copernicus' theory that Earth circles the Sun. Yet he disagreed with it, partly because it did not fit his own careful observations.

The **Ptolemaic system** predicted the paths of the planets with almost complete precision. To achieve anything like the same precision, Copernicus had to add **epicycles**, and so undermined his system's beautiful simplicity. For this reason, Brahe dismissed the idea of a moving Earth. But his young assistant, Johannes Kepler (1571–1630), was not so sure.

When Brahe died in 1601, Kepler took over Brahe's vast store of observations of the night sky and tried to work out why Copernicus' ideas did not quite work. He soon realized that Copernicus was basically right but had made a few crucial errors. Copernicus assumed that the planets move in perfect circles at a constant speed, and that the Sun is perfectly central. Kepler saw that if you abandoned these assumptions, the **Copernican system** could actually be much more accurate than the Ptolemaic system.

In a brilliant feat of mathematics, Kepler worked out that the planets' paths are not quite circular. Instead, they trace a special kind of oval called an **ellipse**. The Sun is also slightly off-centre, and the planets vary their speed – getting faster as they swing nearer the Sun, and slowing down as they swing away again.

TYCHO BRAHE'S STORY

After his nose was cut off in a duel, Tycho Brahe had it replaced with one made of brass, coloured to match his face. It is said that his observations were very accurate because he could take off his false nose to press his eye closer to his instruments.

This portrait of the German astronomer Johannes Kepler was painted in 1627.

Kepler gradually developed a series of mathematical laws to plot the planets' movements. Kepler's laws work so well that astronomers still use them today when calculating how distant galaxies move.

Many astronomers soon realized that Kepler's laws were very good for making accurate predictions. Yet few believed that they gave a true picture of the Universe. Indeed, some astronomers found the idea that planets move in anything but perfect circles quite laughable.

Even though his theories would later upset the Catholic Church a great deal, Johannes Kepler believed he was revealing the perfection of God's plan for the Universe. After his great discovery, he is said to have shouted out, "Oh, Almighty God, I am thinking Your thoughts after You!"

THAT'S AMAZING!

Not all Kepler's ideas were good. He came to believe that the planets resonated as they circled, giving out a low hum. He thought that each planet hummed at a different pitch, depending on the length of its orbit.

Galileo's telescope

These are two of the telescopes through which Galileo made his breakthrough discoveries of Jupiter's moons and Venus' phases. He called them spyglasses. It was only later that they came to be called telescopes.

Kepler showed that Copernicus' idea that Earth moves could work as a theory. Yet few astronomers believed it was actually true. They needed proof, and that was just what the great Italian scientist Galileo Galilei (1564–1642) gave them in 1610.

Scientific theories have to be taken seriously if they make a prediction that proves to be true. Copernicus predicted that, if he was right, the planet Venus would go through **phases** like the Moon's as it circles the Sun. The Moon's phases are the way it seems to change shape from new moon to full moon. This is because, as the Moon moves around Earth, we see different amounts of it lit by the Sun. Unfortunately, Venus is far too distant for any phases to be seen with the unaided eye.

Then, in 1609, Galileo came across a novelty eyeglass called a perspecillium. It was invented in Holland and it used two lenses to make distant objects look bigger. Inspired, Galileo made a much better version that made things look 10 times bigger. This was the first proper telescope.

Proving Copernicus right

Galileo turned his telescope on to the night sky and was amazed. He saw that the Moon is not the perfect sphere it was then supposed to be, but has mountains and valleys. He also saw that Jupiter is not perfectly alone, but is circled by four moons. These are now known as the Galilean moons.

TVBVM OPTICVM VIDES GALILAEI INVENTVM, ET OPVS, QVO SOLIS MACVLAS
ET EXTIMOS IVNAE MONTES, ET IOVIS SATELLITES, ET NOVAM QVASI
RERVM VNIVERSITATE PRIMVS DISPEXIT A. MDCIX.

In 1610, Galileo discovered that Jupiter is circled by moons. He only saw four moons at that time. But Jupiter is now known to have around 60 smaller moons besides the ones that Galileo saw. Some of the recently discovered moons are very tiny indeed – not more than about 1.6 kilometres (1 mile) in diameter.

Finally and crucially, Galileo noticed that Venus does go through the phases that Copernicus predicted, as our view from Earth changes. Venus' phases proved to Galileo and, in time, to most other astronomers that Copernicus was right. Earth is not fixed but circles the Sun, along with the other planets.

The four moons Galileo saw in 1610 are now called Io, Europa, Callisto, and Ganymede. Astronomers have since discovered about 60 other moons of Jupiter.

Jupiter

Io

Europa

Callisto

Ganymede

WHY DID THE CHURCH DISAGREE WITH GALILEO?

The Catholic Church was willing to admit that Copernicus' ideas were a useful theory for making astronomical predictions. Galileo insisted that they were not just a theory but the truth. This was a direct challenge to the leaders of the Church, implying that they did not know the truth. The Pope banned Copernicus' book and warned Galileo not to talk about it. Galileo was not easily silenced. He wrote a book called *The Dialogue* in which a clever character called Sagredo argues with a foolish character called Simplicio about Copernicus. It seemed that Simplicio was the Pope. Galileo was summoned to Rome and forced to deny, maybe under torture, that Earth moves. Legend has it that, as he was led away to be imprisoned in his own house, he muttered, *"eppur si muove"* (*"yet it does move"*).

Discovering gravity

By the mid-17th century, most serious thinkers agreed that Earth moves round the Sun, as Copernicus said. They agreed too that Kepler's laws described the movement of the planets very well. Yet there were two great questions that remained unanswered.

The first question was just why Kepler's laws worked. The second was much older. It was not ignorance that made the ancient Greeks dismiss Aristarchus' idea that Earth moved. It was because they could not see how people would not fall off a moving Earth. Even Galileo could not readily answer this. Then, in 1665, the great English scientist Sir Isaac Newton (1642–1727) had a brilliant insight – **gravity**.

Newton is said to have got the idea sitting in his garden at Woolsthorpe in Lincolnshire, watching an apple fall from a tree. What if the apple was not just falling, Newton wondered, but being pulled by an invisible force? Could this force be what held everything to Earth while it whirled through space? With true genius, Newton realized that this same force, which he called gravity, might also be what keeps the planets circling the Sun. Just as gravity pulls the apple to Earth, so it keeps the Moon circling Earth, and the planets circling the Sun.

Sir Isaac Newton was one of the greatest scientists of all time. His theory of gravity and his laws of motion have shaped our ideas about the Universe ever since.

The theory of gravity

From this simple but brilliant idea, Newton went on to develop a theory of gravity – a universal force of attraction that tries to pull all matter together. With mathematical proofs, he showed that this force exists everywhere. The strength of gravitational attraction depends on how heavy and how far apart objects are.

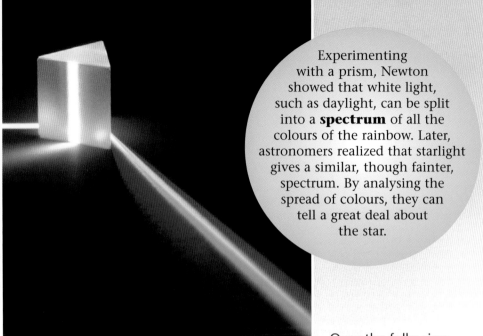

Experimenting with a prism, Newton showed that white light, such as daylight, can be split into a **spectrum** of all the colours of the rainbow. Later, astronomers realized that starlight gives a similar, though fainter, spectrum. By analysing the spread of colours, they can tell a great deal about the star.

Over the following 20 years, Newton refined his theory of gravity into a complete system that included three famous laws of motion. Together, these laws have given astronomers a mathematical framework for analysing and predicting how everything in the Universe moves. Although Albert Einstein (1879–1955) would add a crucial refinement 250 years later (see page 27), it is Newton's laws that still underpin most astronomical calculations.

? WHY DO PLANETS STAY IN ORBIT?

Newton realized that planets stay in orbit around the Sun because of a balance between gravity and **inertia**. Inertia is the tendency for things to stay still or keep moving at the same speed in a straight line. The planets' inertia keeps them flying on through space. The gravitational pull between each planet and the Sun holds them in orbit. Gravity and inertia are in perfect balance. If the inertia were too great or the gravity too weak, the planets would fly off into space, away from the Sun. If the inertia were too weak and the gravity too strong, the planets would spiral into the Sun.

New planets, distant stars

Following Galileo, the telescope became the astronomer's standard equipment. Yet major discoveries were rare, until the arrival of another great astronomer in the 1780s.

Born in Germany, William Herschel (1738–1822) moved to England in 1757. There he took up astronomy and started building increasingly powerful telescopes. For thousands of years, astronomers only knew the five planets that were visible to the unaided eye: Mercury, Venus, Mars, Jupiter, and Saturn. In 1781, Herschel identified a sixth planet. He called it "George's Star" after King George III, but it was eventually named Uranus.

William Herschel is shown here looking through a telescope while his sister Caroline takes notes. Caroline was a brilliant astronomer in her own right, discovering eight comets.

How far to the stars?

Soon Herschel began to try and work out how far away the stars are. The dimmer a star looks, Herschel thought, the further away it must be. We now know that this does not work. Some stars burn brilliantly while others glimmer faintly, so a dim star might be far away or it might just glow feebly. Nevertheless, Herschel's method was a start. He compared each star's brightness to Sirius, the brightest star, and then calculated its distance in siriometers (that is, how it compared to the distance to Sirius).

Using this method, Herschel built up a rough three-dimensional map of the stars. He found that most were clustered in a thick pancake along the bright band in the night sky. This pancake soon became known as the Milky Way.

Then in 1838, for the first time, German astronomer Friedrich Bessel (1784–1846) worked out the actual distance to a star – 61 Cygni. He did this by measuring how its position against other stars shifts slightly through the year. This method is called **parallax**. The answer he came up with was shockingly big. Even though 61 Cygni is one of the nearest stars, Bessel estimated that it was 100 trillion kilometres (60 trillion miles) away. That is 720,000 times further than the Sun!

There was an even greater shock to come. Bessel's measurement told astronomers how big a siriometer was, so they could now work out the distances to all the stars in Herschel's map. They soon realized that the furthest stars in the Milky Way were over 1,000 times further away even than 61 Cygni. Suddenly the Universe seemed very, very big.

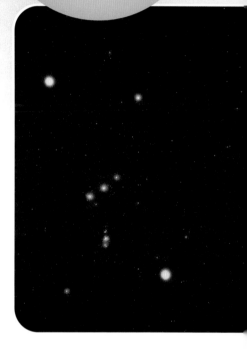

Astronomers still estimate distance by comparing the brightness of stars. But they have to take into account a star's true brightness, indicated by its colour. For instance, each of these stars is at a very different distance.

WHAT WERE THE UNIDENTIFIED LIGHTS IN THE SKY?

Telescopes revealed a host of smudges of light called **nebulae**, as well as stars. French astronomer Charles Messier (1730–1817) began to list the lights by number in a catalogue. Herschel identified thousands more. Yet no one knew what they were. The philosopher Immanuel Kant (1724–1804) believed most of them were giant clusters of stars far beyond the Milky Way. It turned out that he was right, but few agreed with him at the time. Today, astronomers use the word "nebula" differently to describe giant clouds of gas and dust in space.

Discovering more planets

Herschel's discovery of Uranus was a great breakthrough. Yet it soon began to throw up problems for astronomers. Uranus kept appearing in places where it should not be, according to Newton's and Kepler's laws. Was there another, even more remote planet beyond Uranus that was disturbing Uranus' orbit with the pull of its gravity?

Using Newton's maths, young French astronomer Urbain Le Verrier (1811–1877) predicted where this mystery planet might be, based on the disturbances in Uranus' orbit. Le Verrier told astronomers in Berlin, Germany, where to point their telescopes if they wanted to see it. On 23 September 1846, the Berlin astronomers found the mystery planet in just half an hour, exactly where Le Verrier said it would be. Astronomers named the new planet in our **Solar System** Neptune.

WHO DISCOVERED NEPTUNE?

As soon as Le Verrier announced he had found Neptune, British astronomers claimed they already knew about it. According to them, British astronomer John Crouch Adams had worked out where Neptune was; they just had not pointed their telescopes at it yet. A row broke out over who should be credited with the discovery. In the end, both Le Verrier and Crouch Adams were given the credit. Then, in 2004, stolen documents from the time were found in Chile. These revealed the truth. The British astronomers had wildly exaggerated how far Adams had gone in his calculations. In any case, he had actually been ignored by his colleagues.

In 1930, astronomers discovered another planet, Pluto. This brought the Solar System's total up to nine, including Earth. Pluto is very, very far away and very tiny (smaller than the Moon). In January 2005, astronomers discovered another planetlike object, further out than Pluto, but much larger. Rather than call this a planet, astronomers decided that Pluto is not a planet after all. In future, only the Solar System's eight large worlds should be described as planets.

It is not just our Sun that has planets circling it, however. Astronomers estimate that about 30 billion other stars in our galaxy have planets circling them too. Most of these planets are much too far away to see. But they can be detected by a variety of other means, just as Neptune was. The first of these "extrasolar planets" was discovered in 1992. Since then, well over 100 have been identified. Most are at least as big as Jupiter. But astronomers have also found other planets that are more similar in size to Earth, such as planet OGLE–2005–BLG–390Lb, which was discovered in January 2006.

THAT'S AMAZING!

Officially the Solar System's newest planet is called 2003 UB313. But Mike Brown, the astronomer who discovered it, called it Xena after a TV character, Xena the warrior princess. *"I always wanted to name something Xena,"* he said.

In recent years, astronomers have discovered planets orbiting many distant stars. These planets are too far away to see, so this view of a planet near the Trifid nebula is entirely imaginary.

The giant Universe

In 1920, astronomers were divided. On the one side were those who thought the Universe was nothing more than the Milky Way. On the other were those who believed it was much bigger.

The debate focused on **nebulae**, the pale smudges that Messier and Herschel had catalogued in the 18th century. By 1920, powerful telescopes had revealed that many nebulae contained stars. Some astronomers argued that nebulae shine dimly because they are very distant. Nebulae, they said, are actually separate galaxies – giant collections of stars like the Milky Way, but far beyond it. Their opponents countered that nebulae are just pale clusters of stars inside the Milky Way.

The only way to resolve the dispute was to find out how far away nebulae are. With such distant objects, the **parallax** shift used by Bessel in 1838 (see page 17) is too tiny to measure. Instead, the answer lay in a special kind of star called a **cepheid**, discovered in 1784 by John Goodricke (1764–1786). Cepheids regularly get bright, then go dim again. In the early 1900s, American astronomer Henrietta Leavitt (1868–1921) made a great discovery about the way cepheids vary. The brighter the star, the longer the time between brightness peaks.

THAT'S AMAZING!

In 1877, Edward Pickering of Harvard College, in the United States, started to make a complete catalogue of the stars. This meant analysing or "computing" half a million photographs. He recruited a team of men to help, but the men kept on making mistakes. Pickering burst out, "Even my Scotch maid could do a better job!" True to his word, he sacked the men and put his Scottish maid, Williamina Fleming, in charge. She took on a team of women, who proved very good at cataloguing, and made many crucial astronomical discoveries. They included Annie Jump Cannon (1863–1941) and Henrietta Leavitt.

Astronomers saw that Leavitt's discovery could be linked to Herschel's idea that a star's apparent brightness gives a clue to its distance. If one cepheid is dimmer than another cepheid with the same time between brightness peaks, it must be further away. By comparing distances and variation times, you can work out the relative distance of all cepheids.

Astronomers now needed to know the distance to just one cepheid in order to work out the distance to all others. In 1921, American Harlow Shapley and Denmark's Ejnar Hertzsprung found it.

HOW ARE STARS CLASSIFIED?

Between 1911 and 1915, Annie Jump Cannon was working on cataloguing stars. She realized she could classify them into seven groups, according to their colour and brightness. She gave these groups the letters O, B, A, F, G, K, and M. Group O stars are the hottest, brightest, bluest stars. M are the coolest, dimmest, reddest stars. This system of classifying stars is still used today.

Annie Jump Cannon was one of Pickering's team of women cataloguers at the Harvard College Observatory, in the United States. She catalogued over 350,000 stars in total.

Discovering galaxies

Once astronomers could work out the distance to cepheids, they needed to find one in a nebula. This would tell them how far away the nebula was. This great discovery was made by American astronomer Edwin Hubble (1889–1953).

Hubble was working at California's Mount Wilson Observatory, which had the biggest telescope in the world. In October 1923, Hubble was using this giant telescope to photograph the M31 nebula, known as the Andromeda. He photographed the nebula over three nights, and spotted two specks that could only be **nova** (newly created stars). He also found a third speck. This third speck appeared in some photos and not others, so it could only be a variable star. He had found a cepheid in a nebula!

Hubble showed that the Universe is much, much bigger than anyone thought. He also showed that it is getting bigger all the time.

Hubble found that the star took a month to vary in brightness. That meant it must be incredibly bright – 7,000 times brighter than our Sun. Using Leavitt's scale, Hubble worked out how far away it must be. The result was staggering.

Previous estimates put the Milky Way at about 100,000 light years across. Yet Hubble's cepheid in Andromeda was over 900,000 light years away (though we now know it is 2.3 million light years away). This could only mean that Andromeda is not in the Milky Way at all. It is an entirely separate galaxy.

WHAT ARE LIGHT YEARS?

Distances in space are so huge that measuring them in kilometres would give unmanageably large figures. For this reason, astronomers measure them in light years instead. A light year is the distance that light travels in a year. Light travels 299,792 kilometres (186,282 miles) per second. In a year it travels 9,459,724,032,000 kilometres (5,878,000,000,000 miles), which is almost 10 trillion kilometres (6 trillion miles)!

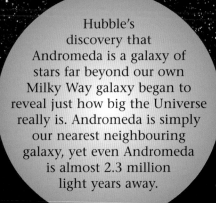

Hubble's discovery that Andromeda is a galaxy of stars far beyond our own Milky Way galaxy began to reveal just how big the Universe really is. Andromeda is simply our nearest neighbouring galaxy, yet even Andromeda is almost 2.3 million light years away.

With a few photographs of a single star, Hubble had shown that the Universe is 100 times bigger than people had ever thought. He became a celebrity overnight.

Before long, astronomers had identified many more galaxies. Although some nebulae were clouds of gas within the Milky Way, most turned out to be faraway galaxies, each filled with millions of stars. We have since discovered that there are billions of galaxies, some over 10 billion light years away. The word "nebula" is now used to describe clouds of dust and gas in our own galaxy.

THAT'S AMAZING!

The most distant galaxy yet observed, which is known as Abell 1835, is 13.2 billion light years away! That means the light astronomers see has taken 13.2 billion years to get here. They are seeing it not as it is now, but as it was 13.2 billion years ago, soon after the Universe was born.

The relative Universe

One person who took a keen interest in Hubble's discovery of galaxies was the great German-American scientist Albert Einstein.

In 1905, Einstein had stunned the scientific world with his **Special Relativity theory**. In this, he built on Galileo's theory that all movement is relative. In other words, you can only tell that you are moving by comparison to something. Galileo described how if you were in a windowless cabin on a smoothly gliding ship, you would have no way of telling if you were moving or not.

Born in Ulm in Germany in 1879, Albert Einstein revolutionized our understanding of the Universe. He not only transformed our view of matter, energy, light, and gravity, but overturned our entire idea of space and time.

Einstein is said to have wondered what would happen to your reflection in a mirror if the ship sailed as fast as light. Would you keep up with the light that forms your reflection? If so, your reflection would vanish because the light would never get back to you fast enough. Then you would know you were travelling at the speed of light. This would surely disprove Galileo's idea.

However, Einstein realized that this is not what happens – because you can never catch up with light, no matter how fast you go. Galileo was right that all movement is relative, but only because light is special. Light is the one speed that is **absolute**, not relative. Einstein called his theory Special Relativity.

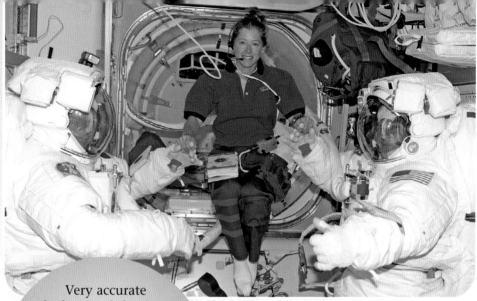

Very accurate clocks reveal that time runs a little slower on a speeding spacecraft, as Einstein's theory predicts. This means that astronauts arrive back from space very slightly younger than if they had stayed on Earth.

Then Einstein realized that if the speed of light is fixed, something else has to be changeable, and that must be time and space. In other words, time and space vary instead of the speed of light.

We do not notice the effects of these time and space variations in everyday life. This is because we are all moving through time and space at pretty much the same speed. However, later experiments showed that these effects are real. When things are moving at the enormous speeds common in space, the effects can be dramatic.

WHAT HAPPENS NEAR THE SPEED OF LIGHT?

Einstein's theory showed that some strange things must go on when objects are travelling very fast. Imagine watching a spaceship accelerating to near the speed of light. Everything in the ship would seem completely normal to the astronauts. But, from Earth, you would notice three things.

1) The spaceship would get shorter.

2) Clocks on the spaceship would run slower as time stretched. This is called time dilation.

3) If you could measure it, you would find that the spaceship would grow heavier.

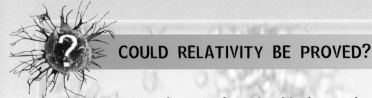

COULD RELATIVITY BE PROVED?

Einstein suggested a way of proving his theory about gravity. He said astronomers should look for a slight shift in the apparent position of a distant star as the Sun passes in front of it. Such a shift would show that the star's light rays were being bent by the warping of **spacetime** close to the Sun. In May 1919, two teams, led by Sir Arthur Eddington, went to Guinea and Brazil to observe an eclipse (the only time when stars can be seen close to the Sun). The teams' photographs showed a star appearing to shift just as Einstein predicted.

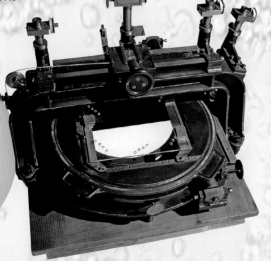

This is the instrument Eddington used to measure a slight shift in a star's position close to an eclipse in 1919, in his attempt to prove Einstein's theory.

Bending space

In his Special Relativity theory, Einstein showed that time and space are inseparably linked. We tend to think of time as something completely separate. Yet Einstein recognized that you move through time just as you move through space. This was how Herman Minkowski (1864–1909) came up with the idea of spacetime. Spacetime has four dimensions – the three dimensions of space, plus time as the fourth.

Einstein's Special Relativity theory worked for objects that move at a steady speed. Using the idea of spacetime, Einstein developed his **General Relativity theory** in 1915. In this theory, he explored what happens to objects that change speed or direction. As he did so, he came up with an entirely new idea of **gravity**.

Here is an imaginary view of how the fabric of spacetime, shown by the grid of orange lines, is warped by gravity.

According to Einstein, gravity is not a force (as Newton said it was). It is a distortion in spacetime that is created by the presence of mass and energy. Scientists often visualize spacetime as a sheet of stretchy fabric. Imagine putting a large mass, such as the Sun, on the "fabric" of spacetime. It will warp to form a hollow, just as a trampoline might if you put a heavy bowling ball on it. If you then add a smaller, lighter mass, such as Earth, it will run down into the hollow created by the Sun. Only Earth's momentum keeps it from falling altogether.

The implications of Einstein's theory were huge. Newton's gravity works for normal situations, but Einstein's theory also works in situations where gravity is extreme. In the vastness of the Universe, extremes are common.

THAT'S AMAZING!

Mercury has a slight apparent wobble in its orbit that is not quite explained by Newton's laws. In the 1800s, astronomers wondered if there might be a small, unseen planet near the Sun disturbing Mercury's orbit. They called the mystery planet Vulcan, though no one could find it. Then Einstein calculated Mercury's orbit in line with General Relativity, and found a perfect fit. There was no need to look for Vulcan any more. Close to the giant mass of the Sun, gravity is so extreme that Newton's laws do not quite work – but Einstein's do.

The expanding Universe

Edwin Hubble's discovery of galaxies and Albert Einstein's 1915 **General Relativity** completely overturned our picture of the Universe. But there was an even more dramatic discovery to come.

Once Einstein had developed his theories of relativity, he wanted to apply his ideas to the **cosmos** (that is, the whole Universe). Making calculations for the whole Universe would be an impossibly large task, so he assumed that it is the same everywhere. Then he only needed to work on a small area.

Einstein's theories showed that gravity warps **spacetime**. Other scientists soon began to wonder how this would work over the whole Universe, and what shape it would make space. One idea was that space would be shaped like a doughnut, with the visible Universe papered along the inside.

Einstein was unhappy with the results of his calculations. They implied that **gravity** pulls every object in the Universe together. Things might only creep together at first. But sooner or later they would rush together like an avalanche, ending the Universe in one gigantic crunch. This could not be right. Surely the Universe was eternal and unchanging? So Einstein added to his sums a figure for a force that counteracts the effect of gravity by pushing things apart. He called this figure the **cosmological constant**.

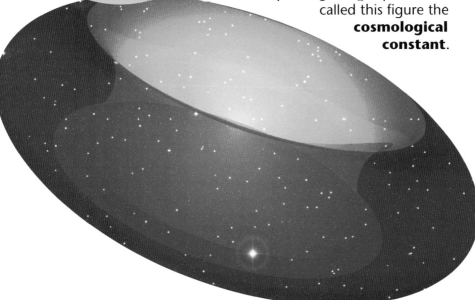

Alexander Friedmann suggested that the fate of the Universe depends on how much matter it contains. If it is quite dense, he thought, then gravity will eventually overcome the expansion. The Universe will then start to collapse. If the density is low, it will expand forever. If the density is in between, the expansion will slow down but never quite stop. Scientists today agree with this analysis, but cannot yet tell which is the case.

Georges Lemaître was the Belgian priest whose theory that the Universe started with a single exploding atom was the forerunner of today's Big Bang model.

Einstein's cosmological constant worked, but he knew it was a "cheat". In 1922 Alexander Friedmann (1888–1925), a young Russian mathematician, explored what would happen if there were no force such as that suggested by the cosmological constant. If so, the only reason the Universe was not collapsing could be because it was being flung apart. Friedmann thought that the Universe had started as a tiny point, then expanded. Its expansion was counteracting gravity, just like a ball flung in the air.

The idea that the Universe could change was revolutionary – so revolutionary that even Einstein dismissed it. Then three years later, in 1925, a young Belgian priest called Georges Lemaître (1894–1966) independently came up with a similar idea. Like Friedmann, he believed that the General Relativity theory was right and the cosmological constant wrong. Lemaître suggested that, long ago, all the stars were squeezed together in one gigantic atom. This single atom split and spread out to form the Universe we know today. Again, Einstein dismissed the idea. He was soon to regret his haste.

Runaway galaxies

Back in 1842, Austrian scientist Christian Doppler (1803–1853) recognized an effect that is very familiar today. If you stand near a busy road, you hear car engines going "eeeyoooow". The sound rises in pitch as they approach, then drops as they move away. Doppler realized why effects like these occur. Sound waves from things coming nearer are squashed, like a boat's bow wave. As they move away, sound waves are stretched out in their wake.

These three diagrams show how the **spectrum** of a star's light shifts, depending on its position and movement. The shift is shown as a particular line in the spectrum moves towards the red end or the blue end.

Doppler thought this would work with light waves as well as sound. In 1868, English astronomers William and Margaret Huggins discovered they could use it to work out whether stars are moving towards or away from Earth. If a star is moving towards Earth, the light is compressed and becomes slightly bluer. This is called a **blue shift**.

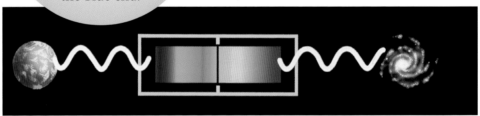

1) Star staying still in relation to Earth

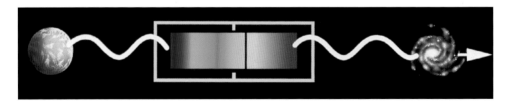

2) Star moving away, causing a red shift as light waves are stretched

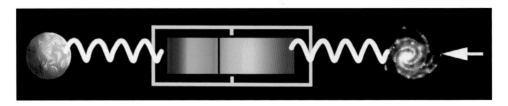

3) Star moving towards Earth, causing a blue shift as light waves are squeezed

If a star is flying away, its light is stretched out and becomes slightly redder. This is a **red shift**. The greater the red shift, the faster the star must be moving.

Between 1912 and 1917, American astronomer Vesto Slipher studied the light from 25 **nebulae**. He found that most are red shifted and so moving away from Earth. As soon as Hubble discovered that most nebulae are really galaxies, he decided to find out what was going on. Aided by photographer Milton Humason, he analysed the red shifts of many galaxies. By 1931, they had completed their analysis – and the results rocked the world of astronomy.

It was clear that a galaxy's red shift varies with its distance from Earth. The further away the galaxy, the more it is red shifted, and the faster it is moving. The most distant galaxies seemed to be hurtling away at almost a tenth of the speed of light!

This could only mean one thing. Instead of being stable and eternal, the Universe was expanding, and expanding rapidly. It was exactly as Friedmann and Lemaître had said. Einstein was the first to admit his mistake.

THAT'S AMAZING!

You might think that if the galaxies are all racing away from us, then we must be at the centre of the Universe. This is not so. Wherever you were in the Universe, you would see galaxies racing away from you in the same way. This is because the galaxies are not actually moving through space. Instead, the space between them is expanding. To see how this works, stick some stars on a half-inflated balloon to represent the galaxies. Then blow up the balloon a little more. You will see the stars getting further apart as the balloon (or space) gets bigger – but they stay in the same place on the balloon (or in space).

Redating the Universe

Astronomers were divided over Hubble's discovery that the Universe is expanding. Some thought it proved that Friedmann was right. If the Universe is expanding, it must have been smaller once. If you wind back the clock far enough, you get to a tiny point – the beginning of the Universe. It was as if the Universe had begun with a mighty explosion, from which the galaxies are still hurtling even today. Eventually, this theory came to be called the **Big Bang**.

Other astronomers were not sure this was right. One big problem was that Hubble's figures suggested that the Universe is expanding so fast it could only be 1.8 billion years old. This was impossible. Scientists already knew that Earth is over 4 billion years old. Earth could not be older than the entire Universe.

New stars are constantly being born inside huge gas clouds, such as those in the pink regions of this spiral galaxy NGC 6946. Meanwhile, other stars reach the end of their lives. The largest stars die in massive explosions (called supernovae), eight of which have been identified in this galaxy.

Another problem was that the Big Bang theory could not explain how all the different chemical elements came to exist. Over the next 20 years, astronomers argued furiously about it.

In 1946, a trio of scientists in England, Fred Hoyle (1915–2001), Thomas Gold (1920–2004), and Hermann Bondi (1919–2005), came up with another idea. This came to be known as the **Steady State theory**. Hoyle, Gold, and Bondi disagreed that the Universe had begun small, then expanded ever outwards. They insisted that the red shifts of the galaxies simply indicate the continual expansion of space between the galaxies. But, as the space between the galaxies expands, they argued, so it fills up with new matter. If the Universe is infinite, and the same thing is happening everywhere, this means the Universe never actually changes.

The argument raged on, but the Big Bang theory got a boost when astronomers began to look again at the distances of the galaxies. In 1952, German astronomer Walter Baade showed that Hubble had compared the wrong type of **cepheids** and so vastly underestimated the distance of the galaxies. If so, the Universe must be twice as old. Over the next 10 years, Baade's student Allan Sandage showed that even Baade underestimated the distances. By 1960, astronomers knew that the most distant galaxies were over 10 billion light years away. The Universe was at least 10 billion years old, more than old enough to contain a 4.6 billion-year-old Earth.

TALKING SCIENCE

The Cambridge astronomer Fred Hoyle was the Big Bang theory's biggest critic. Yet it was he who gave it the name "the Big Bang". On a BBC radio broadcast in 1950, he was talking about rival theories of the Universe. One idea, he explained, was that, *"the Universe started its life a finite time ago in a single huge explosion... Now this Big Bang idea seemed to me to be unsatisfactory."* Although he meant the name as an insult, it was so memorable that it stuck!

Making the Universe

Big Bang theory said the Universe started as nothing. Scientists who favoured this theory had to explain how all the chemicals in the Universe came to exist.

Russian-born American George Gamow (1904–1968) and American Ralph Alpher (1921–) decided to work out what happened in the first moments of the Universe. If you use a bicycle pump, it gets warm as the air is squeezed. In the same way, the Universe must have been hotter when it was more compact, early in its life.

Gamow and Alpher worked out exactly how hot the early Universe must have been. It was so hot that matter, as we know it, could not have existed.

? HOW DOES THE UNIVERSE MAKE ATOMS?

The Universe builds atoms – and so new chemical elements – by forcing atomic nuclei together in new combinations. This is called **nuclear fusion**. It is the same process that powers hydrogen bombs and stars. Light elements, such as hydrogen and helium, were formed by nuclear fusion on a gigantic scale, early in the Universe's life. Heavier elements, such as carbon and iron, were forged by nuclear fusion deep inside stars and by exploding stars called **supernovae**.

This is a computer illustration of a nuclear fusion reaction. The nuclei (central cores) of smaller atoms, such as hydrogen and helium, fuse together to make new atoms.

There were no atoms. Instead, there was an incredibly hot, dense soup of the particles from which atoms are made. The first atoms must have been hydrogen and helium. These are the simplest and smallest atoms. They also make up 99.99 per cent of the atoms in the Universe. All the other, bigger, more complex atoms were probably made when hydrogen and helium combined in different ways.

For the particles to fuse into atoms, the Universe had to expand and cool – but only a little. Once it cooled too much, it would be too cool for atoms to form. In fact, Gamow and Alpher calculated that it took no longer than 5 minutes for all the hydrogen and helium atoms in the Universe to form.

New stars form in inky clouds such as this one. In the fingers of the cloud, gravity drags globules of matter together. The matter eventually becomes so compressed that nuclear fusion occurs, and a new star is born. Gravity created the first galaxies in this way, early in the Universe's life.

With Robert Herman, Alpher worked out that after this critical first 5 minutes the Universe went on expanding and cooling. Although it was soon too cool for atoms to fuse, it was still incredibly hot. It formed a **plasma**, a state of matter so hot that atoms cannot hold on to their **electrons**.

The Big Bang plasma was a sea of light. Yet this light was scattered so much by loose electrons that it was effectively a fog. Only when the Universe expanded and cooled down did the electrons attach themselves to atoms. At that point, the fog lifted, and light rays could travel unhindered throughout the Universe. Both Alpher and Herman believed that this happened when the Universe was about 300,000 years old.

Signs of the Big Bang

In 1960, astronomers were still divided between **Big Bang** and **Steady State theory** supporters. But over the next dozen years, three key discoveries were to shift the balance in favour of the Big Bang.

The first was the discovery of astonishingly bright and very distant galaxies called quasars. Quasars are a very special type of radio galaxy. Radio galaxies beam out mostly radio waves rather than light. They were discovered in the 1950s, when astronomers first realized that stars might send out natural radio signals.

Radio galaxies are believed to form before most other galaxies. If the Steady State theory were right, some radio galaxies would be close to us (because the Steady State theory suggests that galaxies form equally everywhere). Alternatively, if the Big Bang theory were right, then they should all be further away. As signals from the furthest parts of the galaxy take longest to reach us, they must date from early in the Universe's history. In 1961, Cambridge astronomer Martin Ryle found that most radio galaxies tend to be quite a long way from Earth. This was a good piece of evidence in favour of the Big Bang.

This 1965 photograph shows a radio telescope near Cambridge, in the United Kingdom. Professor Martin Ryle (front centre, right) found that most radio galaxies are far away and must date from the early days of the Universe.

In 1963, there was a much more dramatic discovery. An astronomer called Martin Schmidt was studying radio galaxy 3C 273. It beamed out a very strong signal. It also shone brightly enough to be seen with an ordinary telescope. Radio sources were normally distant galaxies. But 3C 273 was so strong and bright that Schmidt at first thought it must be a nearby star.

Then Schmidt did a **red shift** test. The results were astonishing – 3C 273 was actually zooming away from Earth at one-sixth of the speed of light. No one had ever seen anything move this fast before. Schmidt worked out that it was the most distant object ever seen, over 1 billion light years away. It was not a nearby star at all. It was actually a distant galaxy, shining hundreds of times brighter than any known galaxy.

This is quasar PG00052+251, which is about 1.4 billion light years away. It is surrounded by a spiral galaxy of stars. The quasar is actually the brilliant light that shines out as countless stars are sucked into the supermassive **black hole** at the heart of the galaxy.

Astronomers called 3C 273 a quasar. They soon found several more quasars that were even more distant and brilliant. The discovery of such distinctive galaxies right on the fringes of the Universe was further powerful evidence in favour of the Big Bang.

? WHAT DOES QUASAR MEAN?

Quasar is short for "quasi-stellar radio object". Stellar means "star-like". The name comes from the fact that, although quasars are actually distant galaxies, they are so bright they look like nearby stars.

Echoes of the Big Bang

Back in the 1940s, Alpher and Herman had worked out that if there was a Big Bang the early Universe must have been flooded with a fog of light. The fog finally cleared about 300,000 years after the Big Bang. But Alpher and Herman believed that such a strong flood of light should still leave a faint glow today. They thought that this glow would not be visible light. Instead, its waves would have been stretched out into microwaves. If faint microwaves were ever detected coming from all directions, the two astronomers argued that this would be very good evidence for the Big Bang.

No one followed this idea up. But then, in the 1960s, Arno Penzias and Robert Wilson started to work with a radio telescope at the Bell Laboratories in New Jersey, in the United States. A radio telescope is essentially a radio receiver that tunes into radio signals from the skies. Before getting down to serious work, Penzias and Wilson were anxious to get rid of any interference, since the signals from radio galaxies are very faint. Annoyingly, they found a constant slight fuzz of "white noise", like the hiss you get on a radio when you move between stations.

The engineers at the Bell Laboratories in New Jersey combined their astronomical research with development of telecommunications technology. This scoop-shaped telephone and television aerial was photographed there in 1954.

The two researchers were desperate to get rid of this fuzz. At one time, they thought pigeon droppings were to blame. They became skilled at shooting pigeons. But it was not the pigeons at all, as they eventually realized.

In 1964, an astronomer told them about an idea he had heard. Apparently, two Princeton University astronomers, Robert Dicke and James Peebles, had worked out that the Big Bang would have left a microwave signal. They called it the **Cosmic Microwave Background (CMB)**. Dicke and Peebles were unaware that Alpher and Herman had suggested this 15 years earlier. Hearing about CMB, Penzias and Wilson realized at once what their fuzzy noise was. It was the faint echo of the Big Bang, coming from all over the sky.

While using this aerial at Bell Laboratories, Penzias and Wilson unexpectedly discovered the Universe's microwave background radiation. This provided vital evidence for the Big Bang.

THAT'S AMAZING!

Visible **radiation** (the light we can see) is not the only radiation beamed out by stars and galaxies. They also emit invisible rays, such as X-rays and radio waves. These can be detected with special telescopes, revealing far more about space than would be possible with visible light alone. Radio telescopes are huge dishes that pick up natural radio signals pumped out by certain stars and galaxies. Radio astronomy allows astronomers to see into the heart of the clouds where stars are born.

Seeing the beginning

When Penzias and Wilson discovered the CMB, most astronomers were convinced that it was the lingering glow of the Big Bang. Yet there remained a doubt. The CMB appeared completely smooth and even. If there are no variations, how could stars and galaxies ever have formed? If the CMB really is the afterglow of Big Bang, astronomers would expect to see little ripples. Without these ripples to start with, the structures of the Universe could never have developed.

Telescopes taken up above Earth's atmosphere on space satellites have revealed an enormous amount about the Universe. This is the famous Hubble space telescope, launched in 1990.

WHY PUT TELESCOPES IN SPACE?

Looking at space through Earth's atmosphere is rather like looking through a frosted-glass window. This is why astronomers put telescopes in space, on satellites orbiting the Earth, where they can get a clearer view. Many telescopes have now been sent up into space.

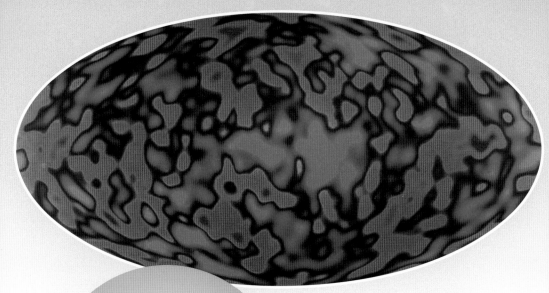

This is a map of the whole sky, in every direction. It shows the slight temperature variations in the Cosmic Microwave Background (CMB) plotted with data from the COBE satellite. Computer analysis of these variations discovered slight ripples, providing strong evidence in favour of the Big Bang theory.

Californian astronomer George Smoot was determined to detect the ripples. However, the ripples are so faint that any sign of them would be swamped by variations in Earth's atmosphere. To get beyond the atmosphere, Smoot sent up detectors in balloons in the 1970s, then high-flying spyplanes. When none of these found any variation in the CMB at all, Smoot realized the only way to get a clear view was to send his detectors into space on a satellite.

TALKING SCIENCE

Reaction to the news of the COBE results was dramatic. George Smoot said, *"...it's like seeing the face of God."* The famous British scientist Stephen Hawking said, *"It's the discovery of the century, if not of all time."* The *Newsweek* magazine headline was: *"The Handwriting of God."*

After a number of setbacks, Smoot and his team finally got their Cosmic Background Explorer (COBE) satellite launched in 1989. It took two years for COBE to scan the entire sky, mapping all the microwave signals. It took a further four months to analyse the results. Finally, on 23 April 1992, Smoot announced the team's results to the world. They had found what they were looking for. The ripples were very, very subtle, but they were definitely there.

Black holes and the Big Bang

Newton's **gravity** works for most everyday events. But Einstein's **General Relativity theory** suggested that things work completely differently under extreme gravity conditions.

In 1916, German astronomer Karl Schwarzschild (1873–1916) used Einstein's theory to show what happens when a big star has burned up all its nuclear fuel. The star collapses under the influence of its own gravity, becoming denser and denser. Eventually, it becomes so dense and its gravity so extreme that nothing, not even light, can escape. It then becomes a **black hole** in space.

Few astronomers took much interest in black holes, until in the 1960s two young English scientists, Roger Penrose and Stephen Hawking, developed a theory about them. In every black hole, they said, there is a rim of no return called the **event horizon**. Beyond this, time has no meaning and light cannot escape. At the heart of the hole is a minute point called a **singularity**. In a singularity, they said, time and all forces become one.

In 1967, the discovery of tiny, super-dense stars called pulsars got some people thinking that black holes might be a reality rather than just a theory. Soon scientists began to make some exciting discoveries which showed that black holes are real.

WHAT ARE PULSARS?

In 1967, astronomer Jocelyn Bell picked up intense radio pulses from the stars. They were so regular it almost seemed they must be coming from aliens. For a while, they were jokingly called "little green men" (LGMs). When other LGMs were picked up, it became clear that the culprits were tiny super-dense stars beaming out regular radio pulses as they spin at fantastic speed. They came to be called pulsars. They are super-giant stars that have collapsed to just 10 kilometres (6 miles) across, squeezing atoms into tiny atomic particles called neutrons. These particles are so dense that a single teaspoonful of neutrons would weigh 10 billion tonnes!

This illustration shows a black doughnut-shaped dust cloud surrounding a supermassive black hole. The orange glow comes from the intense heating of gas and dust as it spirals into the hole. Gigantic jets of gas (shown in blue) shoot out from either side of the hole.

Some black holes form when an old giant star explodes as a **supernova**, then collapses back in on itself. Much larger black holes form at the centre of most galaxies, including our own Milky Way. These gigantic black holes are called supermassive black holes. They contain the mass of billions of stars. At the other extreme, scientists have managed to create miniature black holes in huge machines called **particle accelerators**.

Penrose and Hawking began to think about the black hole's singularity. Then Hawking had a brilliant insight. He turned the collapse of a black hole around to look at the origins of the Universe. What if the **Big Bang** was really a black hole in reverse? If so, the Universe must have begun with a singularity. This gave astronomers a mathematical approach for studying the very first moments of the Universe.

Super-expanding Universe

In 1979, American physicist Alan Guth suggested that for a split second after the Universe was born, gravity acted in reverse, pushing things apart. His idea, called inflation, was that this negative gravity inflated space at an incredible rate to a gigantic size – far, far bigger than we can actually see. Imagine a grain of sand ballooning out to the size of the Milky Way Galaxy in one-trillionth of a second. This is still slow by comparison with inflation!

There was none of the matter or forces familiar today in Guth's inflationary Universe, just an energy field powered by negative gravity. But as the Universe expanded, it began to cool. As it cooled, matter and the familiar forces began to condense out. As they did, gravity became the force of attraction we are more familiar with today, and began to put a brake on inflationary super-expansion. It all took a split second.

There are several types of galaxy. They include spiral galaxies such as our Milky Way, which rotate like giant Catherine wheel fireworks. All these giant galaxies were born in the first billion years of the Universe's life.

Inflation theory solves two problems posed by the Big Bang: the horizon problem and the flatness problem. The horizon problem is the way temperatures in the **Cosmic Microwave Background (CMB)** are almost identical wherever you look in space. For the temperatures to be so similar, all these regions of space must once have been in touch. For example, if you keep a glass of hot water and a glass of cold water separate, they stay at different temperatures. Mix them together, and the water ends up uniformly warm. Yet if the Universe expanded gradually, as suggested by standard Big Bang theory, the far reaches of the Universe must always have been too far apart to swap heat. They were, effectively, out of sight of each other, beyond the "horizon". The high-speed swelling of inflation gets round this problem.

The flatness problem stems from Friedmann's suggestion in the 1920s that the shape of space depends on how densely matter and energy are packed in (see page 29). Astronomers' observations imply that space is flat. If so, it must contain a very particular matter/energy density. A fraction more than this critical density and it would curl inwards; a fraction less and it would unfurl outwards. Scientists doubt that ordinary gravity can achieve such a delicate balance. The negative gravity of inflation appears to solve the problem. Inflation stretched out the Universe so fast and so big that what we see simply looks flat, just as the curved Earth looks flat to us on the ground.

THAT'S AMAZING!

Galaxies formed as clumps of matter were pulled together by gravity. Yet the Universe is believed to have been completely uniform in its first moments, so how did the first clumps form? Inflation theory suggests that the clumps began with incredibly minute random variations. Inflation blew these variations up large enough to create the structures from which galaxies developed.

The dark Universe

In the 1930s, Swiss-American scientist Fritz Zwicky (1898–1974) discovered something odd. He was studying the Coma **cluster**, a huge collection of galaxies over 300 million light years away.

The American astronomer Vera Rubin investigated the rotation speeds of spiral galaxies in the 1970s. Her research provided strong evidence for the existence of dark matter.

Just like planets and galaxies, the entire Coma cluster revolves together. But Zwicky found it was whirling round far too fast for the **gravity** of the cluster's visible matter to hold it together. If the galaxies were not to be flung off into space, Zwicky suggested, the Coma cluster must be held together by the extra gravity of a great deal of matter that we simply cannot see. Scientists later called this invisible matter **dark matter**.

For a while, few astronomers took much interest in dark matter. Then, in the 1970s, astronomers such as Vera Rubin and James Peebles began to plot rotation curves for galaxies. Rotation curves are graphs showing the speed at which stars circle at different distances from the centre of a galaxy. According to Kepler's laws, the stars should orbit slower and slower further out from the centre. In fact, stars on the edge of the galaxy were found to be orbiting just as fast as stars near the centre. The only good explanation was that the stars were not at the edge of the galaxy. They were being held within a much larger disc of dark matter.

THAT'S AMAZING!

In one view of dark matter, it cannot cluster into stars, and does not move. Instead, it is like an incredibly thin gas. Stars and planets hurtle through it as if through a fog. Our **Solar System** is roaring through the dark matter fog at over 220 kilometres (140 miles) per second. Since dark matter particles are so tiny, they simply pass straight through us, as Earth carries us round. In fact, a billion dark matter particles pass through you every second!

WHAT ARE MACHOs AND WIMPs?

Some astronomers divide the dark matter in galaxy haloes into MACHOs and WIMPs. MACHOs (Massive Astrophysical Compact Halo Objects) are thought to be mostly **black holes** and burnt-out stars and giant Jupiter-like planets. MACHOs are like ordinary matter that simply does not shine. WIMPs (Weakly Interacting Massive Particles) are a completely unknown form of matter, made of particles that are unknown to science.

We now know that all the stars in each galaxy are embedded in huge haloes of dark matter stretching far beyond the visible edge of the galaxy. The disc of stars is like a scattering of pepper in between the halves of a very big bun of dark matter that we cannot see. In fact, there is probably six or seven times as much dark matter as visible matter. This means that we simply cannot see most of the matter in the Universe. We only know it is there because of the huge effects of its gravity.

Yannick Mellier and his team in France plotted where dark matter (shown in red) occurs in a section of the Universe 1 billion light years long. They worked it out from the way the dark matter's gravity bends light rays from stars (yellow lines).

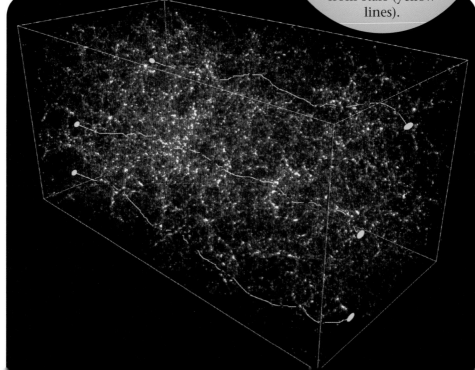

Dark energy

When Einstein worked through the implications of his **General Relativity theory**, he was shocked at what he found. His sums implied that gravity would pull the whole Universe together in a big crunch. To counteract this, he introduced a **cosmological constant**, representing a force that acts against gravity. When Hubble found that the Universe is expanding (see page 22), Einstein was glad to abandon this idea. Like other astronomers, he assumed that the momentum of the **Big Bang** was enough to counteract gravity and keep the Universe swelling.

The ultimate fate of the Universe, astronomers thought, depends on the amount of matter it contains. If it contains more than a certain amount, for instance, its gravity will eventually put a brake on the Universe's expansion. Then it will contract – like a Big Bang in reverse – to a Big Crunch. The discovery of large amounts of dark matter made this seem very likely.

Type 1a supernovae occur when the gas remnants from one old dying star fall on a companion star, triggering a catastrophic, super-bright explosion. They burn with such predictable brightness and so brightly that they can be used as distance markers for distant galaxies.

Then, in 1998, astronomers made a discovery that changed everything. They were studying incredibly bright exploding stars called **supernovae**. What caught their eye were some supernovae called Type 1a.

Type 1a supernovae are so bright they can be seen in the furthest galaxies. They burn briefly but they are always equally bright. This means that it is easy to work out just how far away they are from how bright they look. **Red shifts** show their speeds. When astronomers compared the speed of these supernovae with their distance, they got an astonishing result. It turned out that the expansion of the Universe, far from slowing down, is actually accelerating – and has been for at least the last 7 billion years. It is as if the Universe is blowing itself apart.

Astronomers began to realize that Einstein's cosmological constant is real after all. There is a repulsive force that counteracts gravity. They call this repulsive force **dark energy**. The galaxies are not simply flying apart as space expands. They are being pushed apart by dark energy. The nature of this repulsion is so mysterious that some scientists think it is wrong even to call it "energy". Yet its effects are real. And it seems likely that the Universe will go on expanding until all the matter in it is so stretched out that it dwindles to a cold nothingness.

This is an artist's imaginary view of the early Universe. Galaxies are being pushed outwards by dark energy.

THAT'S AMAZING!

Everyone used to think that if you take all the matter out of space, you are left with nothing – not even space. Some astronomers now believe this is not true. They think "empty space" is in fact dark energy. They also believe that if you put two particles close together in "empty space" the pressure of dark energy would push them apart.

Bringing it all together

Einstein's **General Relativity theory** explains how **gravity** works on a large scale. Einstein predicted that, as masses move, they create ripples in the fabric of **spacetime**. These ripples are called gravity waves. Scientists believe that gravity can take the form of a wave, just like light.

Physicists have discovered that tiny particles carry the other three basic forces in the Universe: **electromagnetism** and the two forces that hold the atomic nucleus together. They are now sure there must also be a **graviton** (a particle for gravity). But gravity is very weak. It is only because planets and stars are so gigantic that it has so much effect.

Particle accelerators are vast circular tunnels where sub-atomic particles are accelerated by electromagnets to enormous speeds, then smashed together. The traces of the smash may reveal a great deal about what these particles are made of. This technician is working in one of the tunnels at the CERN accelerator in Switzerland.

The graviton must be very tiny – so tiny that scientists will probably never detect one. However, they might manage to detect gravity waves. Even so, this is incredibly difficult. Scientists at the CERN laboratory in Switzerland look for gravity waves in collisions between particles accelerated to near the speed of light. They say it is like looking for the movement of a hair between Earth and the Sun.

THAT'S AMAZING!

The most popular candidate for a Theory of Everything involves unimaginably tiny strings of energy called **superstrings**. Literally everything is made from these superstrings. Just as a violin string can make different notes, so a superstring creates all the different particles of matter by vibrating in different ways. But this is an entirely mathematical idea. No one has ever seen a superstring, nor is anyone ever likely to see one.

Finding proof of the graviton will help us understand the four basic forces in terms of an important physics theory called **quantum mechanics**. Quantum mechanics deals with things on the very smallest scale, the size of an atom or less. This is in complete contrast to Relativity, which works on the large scale – the scale of planets, stars, and the whole Universe.

Unfortunately, Relativity and quantum mechanics are totally at odds with each other. Quantum mechanics sees that, on the very smallest scale, things happen in tiny chunks or quanta. On this level, things only happen because they are the most likely things to happen, not because they are certain to happen. This is very different from Relativity and Newton's laws, in which everything happens on a grander scale with mathematical precision and certainty.

Astronomers usually look at things on a large scale, so Relativity is quite adequate. Yet in the first tiny fraction of a second after the Universe began, it was unimaginably tiny. At this time, the Planck Era, quantum ideas must be appropriate. Scientists realize that, to fully understand the story of the Universe, they must find a way to unite Relativity with quantum mechanics. They call this a **Theory of Everything (ToE)**. Many scientists now see finding a ToE as the ultimate quest.

Probing the Big Bang

The **COBE** satellite provided the first detailed picture of the afterglow of the Big Bang, but it was still quite fuzzy. Then, in 2003, data from a new satellite, called the Wilkinson Microwave Anistropy Probe (WMAP), produced a much sharper picture. The picture it provided was so accurate that astronomers could use it to work out the precise age of the Universe for the first time. It turns out to be 13.7 billion years. Surprisingly, the first stars seem to have started shining only 200,000 years after the Big Bang.

The Wilkinson Microwave Anistropy Probe (WMAP) spacecraft was launched in 2001. It is designed to collect microwave **radiation** from every part of the sky. Data from WMAP has enabled scientists to calculate that the Universe is 13.7 billion years old.

Even more amazingly, WMAP provided the first strong indication that **dark energy** is real. Scientists used the WMAP data to work out that the Universe is made up of 4 per cent ordinary matter, 23 per cent **dark matter**, and 73 per cent dark energy. The data also provided firm evidence that the battle between the inward pull of gravity and the outward push of dark energy played a key role in forming the first galaxies.

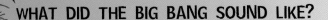

WHAT DID THE BIG BANG SOUND LIKE?

Using the WMAP data, scientists have worked out that the Big Bang was actually more like a deep hum or roar. Physicist John Cramer, of the University of Washington, Seattle, in the United States, has made an audio file recreating the noise. *"The sound is rather like a large jet plane flying 100 feet above your house in the middle of the night,"* he says.

HOW BIG IS THE UNIVERSE?

Is the Universe never-ending, or does it have a definite size? One team of scientists says that WMAP data suggests it has a definite size. It all depends on the biggest ripples detected in the microwave background. Just as waves cannot be bigger than the ocean, so these ripples cannot be bigger than the Universe. If the Universe is infinite, there would be no limit to their size. Yet none of the waves seem to be really big. From the biggest ripples detected, scientists calculate the Universe is "just" 70 billion light years across.

In fact, scientists have found out from WMAP that sound waves were crucial in forming the first galaxies. They believe gigantic sound waves rolled across the early Universe. At the same time, gravity was pulling inwards and radiation was pushing outwards. This process began about 400,000 years after the Big Bang, and lasted about 600,000 years. Like foam on breaking waves, galaxies formed along the leading edge of the sound waves, as they petered out about a million years later.

This map shows the varying temperatures of microwave radiation captured by the WMAP probe. The variations correspond to the time when the Universe became transparent to radiation, 380 million years after the Big Bang.

Dark energy and cosmic ripples

Astronomers now have a very detailed picture of the Universe and how it began. A few scientists think it is about 150 billion light years across. Many others think it is infinite. It is thought to contain around 100 billion galaxies that we can see. The most distant of these is some 13 billion light years away. The galaxies are made of a tiny proportion of visible matter, plus a lot of stuff we cannot see called dark matter. Spread throughout space is a great deal more that we do not even understand called dark energy.

Astronomers think the Universe started from virtually nothing about 13.7 billion years ago. Then, in a process called the Big Bang, it began to swell at a fantastic rate. The speed at which distant **supernovae** are zooming away from us shows it is swelling even faster now than ever before (except during the first brief nanoseconds of inflation). It is driven by the mysterious repulsion that scientists call dark energy.

Only gravity puts a brake on this runaway expansion, tugging matter together to form stars and galaxies. Gravity is by no means a feeble force. It created far more stars in the past than it does now. Yet gravity's compressive power is still strong enough to create the nuclear reactions that keep stars burning. It can also pull galaxies together with such force that they contract into **black holes**.

THAT'S AMAZING!

Scientists are seriously considering the possibility that our Universe may be just one of many. Quantum physics does not allow empty space to exist. In empty space, quantum particles can bubble up out of nothing – because this is just as likely to happen as not. What if the **singularity** that began our Universe is one of these quantum bubbles? If so, lots of Universes could be bubbling into and out of existence all the time, without our knowledge.

Some cosmologists explore the Universe theoretically, with computers and pen and paper, but their theories must also be verified by observations of the real Universe. This telescope at the Yerkes Observatory, in Wisconsin in the United States, is the largest refracting telescope in the world.

Astronomers now have incredibly sensitive equipment, including powerful telescopes both on the ground and on satellites. With this equipment, they can detect the faintest, most distant signals from space. They have detected the faint afterglow of the Big Bang. They have been able to make sensitive tests to indicate the reality of both dark matter and dark energy. With even more sensitive equipment, they hope to trace the indescribably faint ripples of gravity on the move.

Astronomers are determined to find out exactly what the Universe is, and how it came to be. Although we have learned an incredible amount, that goal still seems a long way off.

Timeline

150 BC Hipparchus estimates the distance to the Moon and the Sun.

AD 100 Ptolemy devises his Earth-centred theory of the Universe.

1543 Publication of Nicolaus Copernicus' theory that Earth, along with the other planets, orbits the Sun.

1609 Johannes Kepler shows that the orbits of the planets are elliptical, not circular.

1609–1610 Galileo Galilei uses a telescope to see the surface of the Moon, the phases of Venus, and the moons of Jupiter, providing strong evidence for Copernicus' Sun-centred theory.

1665 Isaac Newton devises theory of gravity as the force that pulls things to the ground and holds the planets in orbit around the Sun.

1769 Charles Messier publishes his catalogue of nebulae.

1781 William Herschel discovers the planet Uranus.

1784 John Goodricke makes the first discovery of a cepheid.

1786 Herschel makes the first estimates of relative distances to the stars.

1838 Friedrich Bessel makes the first estimate of actual distance to a star.

1846 Urbain Le Verrier's predictions enable the discovery of Neptune.

1905 Albert Einstein publishes his Theory of Special Relativity.

1914 Vesto Slipher shows that nebulae are red-shifted and so moving away from Earth.

1915 Annie Jump Cannon publishes the Harvard system for classifying stars.

1915 Einstein publishes his Theory of General Relativity.

1916 Karl Schwarzschild uses Einstein's Theory of General Relativity to develop the theory of black holes.

1921 Harlow Shapley and Ejnar Hertzsprung find the actual distance to a cepheid for the first time.

1922 Alexander Friedmann suggests that the Universe might be expanding from a tiny beginning.

1923 Edwin Hubble makes the first discovery of a galaxy far beyond our own, then reveals that many nebulae are in fact distant galaxies.

1925 Georges Lemaître suggests that the Universe has expanded from a single atom.

1930 The planet Pluto is discovered.

1931 Hubble discovers that the further away a galaxy is, the faster it is moving away from us, showing that the Universe is expanding.

1933 Fritz Zwicky suggests that galaxies may contain invisible matter, later called dark matter.

1946 Fred Hoyle, Thomas Gold, and Hermann Bondi devise the Steady State theory.

1948 George Gamow and Ralph Alpher work out that the Universe began with a very hot, dense soup of particles.

1949 Alpher and Robert Herman work out that the Universe cleared from a dense fog of light about 300,000 years after it began, and that this fog might have left a very faint glow of microwave radiation.

1952–1960 Walter Baade and Allan Sandage show that the Universe is at least 10 billion years old.

1964 Arno Penzias and Robert Wilson pick up the Cosmic Microwave Background (CMB).

1967 Jocelyn Bell discovers the existence of pulsars.

1970 Vera Rubin finds evidence for the existence of dark matter.

1979 Alan Guth develops Inflation theory.

1992 COBE satellite results map the CMB and show it has variations, as predicted by the Big Bang theory.

1998 Study of Type 1a supernovae shows that the Universe's expansion is accelerating.

2003 WMAP satellite data shows that the Universe is 13.7 billion years old.

2005 Discovery of a possible new planet in the Solar System, 2003 UB313, nicknamed Xena.

2006 After the discovery of Xena, astronomers decide that Pluto and other small objects should no longer be described as planets.

Biographies

These are some of the leading scientists in the story of astronomy.

Nicolaus Copernicus (1473–1543)

Nicolaus Copernicus was the first modern astronomer to suggest that Earth circles the Sun, not the other way round. He was born in Torun, on the Vistula river, in northern Poland. His real name was Mikolaj Kopernik. It was only later in life that he adopted the Latin version of his name, Nicolaus Copernicus, as many scholars and priests did at the time. He became a canon at Frombork Cathedral in Poland. There, he gradually developed his ideas on a Sun-centred Universe. He published them briefly in a small pamphlet in 1514. But his great book, which explained his ideas fully, was not published until 1543 when he was about to die.

Albert Einstein (1879–1955)

Born in Ulm, in Germany, Einstein's genius only slowly became clear. After being rejected from several universities for poor grades, he went to work at the patent office in Bern, Switzerland, in 1902. Within just three years, though, he had written five papers, each of which was to have a great impact on science. The first was his explanation of the way light could create electricity. Another helped prove the existence of atoms. The most important was his Special Relativity theory, which showed how only the speed of light is constant and absolute everywhere, and every other movement is relative. Einstein's theory made links between energy and mass that eventually led to the development of nuclear power and nuclear weapons. By 1915, Einstein had developed these ideas into his General Relativity theory, which gave a revolutionary new explanation of gravity. By the time Einstein moved to the United States in 1933, he was the most famous scientist in the world.

Galileo Galilei (1564–1642)

Born in Pisa, in Italy, Galileo had an original mind from a young age. Soon after graduating from Pisa University, Galileo taught first at Padua and then in Florence, combining his teaching with his scientific studies. He was the first great scientist of the modern age. He pioneered the study of motion, and was the first to suggest that all motion is relative. He studied how gravity made things accelerate. But it was his discoveries in the night sky with a telescope that had the most impact. His discovery of the phases of Venus and the moons of Jupiter provided strong evidence for Copernicus' Sun-centred theory of the Universe. His outspoken championing of Copernicus' ideas brought him into conflict with the Roman Catholic Church.

William Herschel (1738–1822)

Born in Germany, Friedrich Wilhelm Herschel went to England as an oboeist with his father in 1759. When his father left, Herschel stayed on in England and adopted the English name William. He went to Bath as an organist and conductor, where he was joined by his sister Caroline. In 1773, Herschel took up astronomy as a hobby and was soon building his own telescopes. They were far better than any yet made. In 1781, he discovered the planet that came to be called Uranus. With his sister Caroline he made the most extensive catalogue of nebulae and star clusters, and made the first estimates of relative distance to the stars by comparing brightness, a method still used today.

Edwin Hubble (1889–1953)

Born in Missouri, in the United States, Edwin Hubble was the greatest astronomer of the 20th century. After studying for several years at Oxford University in the United Kingdom, Hubble took up astronomy. His early skill earned him a post at the Mount Wilson Observatory, California, in 1919. Within a few years, he had discovered that the Andromeda nebula, as it was then called, was not a cloud within our own galaxy, but an entirely separate galaxy far away. This was the first proof that there are galaxies beyond our own, and Hubble became a celebrity almost overnight. Hubble went on to show that the Universe is expanding by the second.

Isaac Newton (1642–1727)

Born on Christmas day in the village of Woolsthorpe in Lincolnshire, Isaac Newton was the greatest English scientist of all time. His catalogue of discoveries began when he was a young student at Cambridge and showed that all the colours of light are contained in white daylight. When forced to return to Woolsthorpe in 1665 by an outbreak of plague across England, Newton laid the foundations of his theory of gravity and his three great laws of motion, which underpin all modern physics. It was here, too, that he invented the reflecting telescope, which is used by many astronomers today. He returned to Cambridge as a professor in 1669, and remained there until 1687 when he went to London as a Member of Parliament. In 1696, Newton became Master of the Royal Mint, a post he remained in until he died in 1727.

Glossary

absolute independent of anything else

asteroid small rock object that orbits the Sun

Big Bang theory that the Universe began in a super-hot, super-dense spot about 13.7 billion years ago and has been expanding ever since

black hole point in space where matter is so dense that everything, even light, is pulled in by its powerful gravity

blue shift opposite of red shift; squeezing of light waves towards the blue end of the spectrum, which shows that stars and galaxies are moving towards Earth

cepheid star that regularly varies its brightness

cluster group of several thousand galaxies

Copernican system Sun-centred idea of the Universe proposed by Nicolaus Copernicus in the 16th century

Cosmic Microwave Background (CMB) heat left over from the Big Bang

cosmological constant figure introduced by Einstein to counteract the inward pull of gravity

cosmos everything that exists

dark energy mysterious force that seems to be pushing the Universe outwards at an ever-increasing speed

dark matter matter that emits no radiation and so cannot be directly seen

electromagnetism combined force of electricity and magnetism

electron one of the three stable particles in an atom, along with the proton and neutron

ellipse shape that resembles a flattened circle

epicycle small circle rotating inside a big circle

event horizon theoretical boundary around a black hole, beyond which nothing can be known since even light cannot escape

General Relativity theory Einstein's theory, which says that gravity is actually the way in which concentrations of mass and energy warp spacetime

graviton undetected particle carrying gravitational force

gravity force of attraction between all mass and energy

inertia reluctance of an object to slow down, speed up, or change direction

Inflation theory idea that there was a brief period of incredible expansion in the first few fractions of a second of the Universe's life

nebula previously used as the name for any unidentified patch of light in the night sky. Most of these light patches are now known to be other galaxies. Today the word nebula is used to describe a cloudy region of gas and dust within our own galaxy.

nova explosive outburst of a faint star in order to become a visible or "new" star

nuclear fusion way in which atomic nuclei are forced together by intense pressure as in the heart of stars, releasing energy

parallax apparent change in the position of an object relative to another object, when viewed from a different place

particle accelerator gigantic circular tunnel used for accelerating particles to high speeds

phase one of the different shapes that moons and planets appear as they are caught by sunlight at different angles

plasma gas that is so hot that electrons float free from their atoms

Ptolemaic system Earth-centred theory of the Universe developed by Hipparchus and Ptolemy

quantum mechanics study of the interactions of particles, based on the idea that mass, energy, and force all occur in tiny, separate chunks or quanta

radiation emission of electromagnetic energy in rays, waves, or particles

red shift opposite of blue shift; stretching of light waves towards the red end of the spectrum, which shows that stars and galaxies are moving away from Earth

retrograde motion occasional apparent looping back of a planet's path through the sky

singularity theoretical point in space where all matter, energy, and forces are infinitely compressed

Solar System grouping of a Sun, planets, their moons, and all the other objects that orbit the Sun

spacetime combination of time with the three normal dimensions of space

Special Relativity theory Einstein's theory that only the speed of light is constant and absolute everywhere

spectrum full array of different colours contained in light

Steady State theory idea that the expansion of the Universe is balanced by continual creation of new matter, so that the Universe never really changes

supernova death of a giant star in an explosion that briefly burns as brightly as an entire galaxy

Theory of Everything (ToE) theory that aims to combine Relativity and quantum mechanics to explain how mass, energy, and force work throughout the Universe

Further resources

If you have enjoyed this book and want to find out more, you can look at the following books and websites.

Books

Discovery Channel School Science:
The Universe
Jacqueline A. Ball (ed.)
(Gareth Stevens Publishing, 2003)

Eyewitness: Universe
Robin Kerrod
(Dorling Kindersley, 2004)

Faraway Worlds:
Planets Beyond Our Solar System
Paul Halpern
(Charlesbridge Publishing, 2004)

Kingfisher Knowledge:
Stars & Planets
Carole Stott
(Kingfisher, 2005)

The Life and Death of Stars
Ray Spangenburg
(Franklin Watts, 2004)

Observing the Universe
Ray Spangenburg
(Franklin Watts, 2004)

Out-Of-This-World Astronomy
Joe Rhatigan
(Lark Books, 2005)

Scholastic Atlas of Space
Scholastic Reference
(Scholastic Reference, 2005)

Websites

About Space
www.space.com/SPACE.com
Up-to-date and highly
informative site with lots
of multimedia features.

Astronomy for Young People
www.kidsastronomy.com/space_
size.htm
This site has a great demonstration
of just how big the Universe is.

European Space Agency (ESA)
www.esa.int/esaKIDSen/
OurUniverse.html
This site includes clear explanations
of the Big Bang and the birth
of galaxies.

NASA
http://spacekids.hq.nasa.gov/
osskids/
A great site run by NASA, with
lots of information on the latest
space missions.

Wilkinson Microwave
Anistropy Probe (WMAP)
http://map.gsfc.nasa.gov/
m_uni.html
NASA's WMAP site is an
advanced and extremely
comprehensive introduction
to all the latest theories about
the Universe.

Index